HOT SIPS

By
Sherri Eldridge

Illustrations by
Rob Groves

Hot Sips

Published by:
CNE Publications, Inc.
P.O. Box 55
Salisbury Cove, Maine 04672
207-288-8988

ISBN: 1-886862-24-9

First printing: June 1997

PRINTED IN THE UNITED STATES
ON ACID-FREE PAPER

10 9 8 7 6 5 4 3 2 1

The recipes in this book were created with the goal of reducing fat, calories, cholesterol and sodium. They also present a variety of fresh healthy foods, to be prepared with love and eaten with pleasure.

CREDITS:

Cover cotton print border gratefully used as a courtesy of:
Northcott/Monarch Silk, Inc.

Cover Design, Layout and Typesetting: Sherri Eldridge

Front Cover Watercolor and Text Line Art: Robert Groves

PREFACE

Sitting down with a friend, family member, acquaintance, or even a perfect stranger to enjoy a hot drink together has been a special event since the early days of man. A quiet intimacy forms between people as they warm to the hot drinks.

Over the millennium, we have created rituals and specialized equipment in support of this tradition. The Japanese and Chinese present an ancient tea ceremony. The English relish both afternoon and high tea. The Turks and Italians sip and watch at sidewalk cafes. All have become part of the fabric of our lives. The equipment to complete these ceremonies has even been the inspiration for works of art. It has produced the Russian samovar, porcelain cups and teapots, the coffee mill, espresso machine, and the more mundane filters, pots, presses and travel mugs that accompany us in daily travels.

Hot brewed drinks are made from herbs, roots, leaves, berries, fruit, bark and flowers. Primitive man discovered all of these, and our main sources of caffeine - tea, coffee, cola, cocoa and yerba mate.

As a stimulant, caffeinated drinks are often limited to a couple cups a day. Fortunately, there are thousands of herbal teas to take their place, many with medicinal properties. For those who crave the taste of tea or coffee, science has come up with decaffeinated processes. Even without the jolt of the real thing, the fulfilling taste remains. So however you take your coffee and tea, enjoy the hot sips!

CONTENTS

A Perfect Cup of Coffee 7
Espresso 8
Cappuccino & Caffé Latte 9
The Flavor of Coffee 10
Mocha Coffee Cake 11
The Coffee Bean 12
The Decaffeinated Experience 13
Irish Coffee 14
Café Marnier 15
Apricot Scones 16
Tea Time 17
English Tea 18
Mint Tea with Crystallized Ginger 19
Golden Raisin Tea Bread 20
Roses and Cloves Tea 21
Burgundy Tea 22
Orange Pekoe with a Twist 23
Selecting and Brewing Teas 24
Chamomile and Lemon Herb Tea 25
Crumpets 26
Raspberry Tea Syrup & Herbal Tea Honey 27
Hazelnut Hot Cocoa 28
Almond Biscotti 29
Mulled Apple Cider 30
Chai 31

A Perfect Cup of Coffee

The perfect cup of coffee is determined by a personal preference for brewing style and the flavor of the beans. Most brewing styles use 2 tablespoons of grounds for every 6 ounces of water, but this will vary with the coffee and your taste. Always serve coffee immediately after making it. Never reheat it or leave on the burner more than 20 minutes. Clean all equipment regularly. Remove residues from coffee oils by scrubbing the pot with a fresh lemon wedge and salt, rinse well.

The most popular brewing styles are drip, Turkish, French press, percolator, vacuum and espresso. For drip coffees, 195° boiling water is poured through the grounds. Turkish coffee is mixed with sugar and boiled three times. French press or Melior forces the water through the grounds by means of a press after it has steeped. Vacuum brewing forces water into the grounds, then is drawn back into the pot as it cools. Espresso machines heat the water and force it through a filter containing the grounds. Many espresso machines also have a steamer for milk, a handy adaptation for making caffé latte and cappuccino.

Keep coffee beans in the freezer, and only grind as needed. Water for making coffee should be cold, and either filtered or bottled. The grind should be coarse for percolator, medium grind for drip and French Press, fine for vacuum, and very fine for espresso and cappuccino.

Espresso

Espresso is a very small cup, about 1.5 ounces, of very strong coffee, made in either a stove-top espresso maker, or an electric machine. If preparing cappuccino or caffé latte, you will need an espresso maker with a nozzle for steaming milk, or a separate steaming device.

Although espresso does not require a particular coffee bean, the deep rich flavor of espresso is accentuated by a dark "espresso roast." The beans should be very finely ground. For each cup of espresso, lightly pack 2 teaspoons of grounds into the gruppa, or metal cup. Examine the grounds after making the espresso; if too tightly packed there will be dry spots, too lightly packed and the espresso will be weak.

The espresso will come out as a black liquid, with a creamy beige layer on top. A short espresso is made by using the same amount of grounds but stopping the water after about 3 tablespoons. For a double espresso, double the amount of grounds and water.

A sweetened espresso needs sugar, but honey or brown sugar can be used. Numerous flavoring combinations can also be made. To a regular espresso, add ¼ teaspoon extract or a tablespoon prepared syrup of vanilla, hazelnut, almond, irish cream or mint. Other flavors can be made with a tablespoon of chocolate syrup, brandy or rum. Chocolate shavings, cocoa, nutmeg, cinnamon or cardamom can be sprinkled on top, before or after the low-fat whipped cream!

Cappuccino & Caffé Latte

Cappuccino and caffé latte are both made from espresso, steamed milk and the foam from the milk. Non-fat and low-fat milk work fine for steaming and foam. Start with a chilled stainless steel pitcher, filled about one-third full with cold milk. With the machine up to full steam, place nozzle on the surface of the milk and turn steam on. As the milk foams and expands, raise the nozzle to keep it just under the surface of the milk. Reduce the pressure of the steam to keep milk from boiling or overflowing the pitcher. The steamed milk is ready when it is full of very small bubbles, with a nice foam on top.

Cappuccino: Follow directions for a single or double espresso, and add to it an equal amount of steamed milk plus another equal portion of foam from the steamed milk. Sprinkle with cinnamon, nutmeg or sweetened cocoa. Try stirring in vanilla or almond extract, rum, brandy, chocolate or butterscotch syrup. A Cappuccino Royale has whipped cream on top, and usually includes a flavoring. To make a Mochaccino, steam chocolate milk instead of regular milk, proceed as for a regular cappuccino and top with whipped cream and cocoa.

Caffé Latte: Follow directions for a single or double espresso, and add to it an equal amount of steamed milk and just a thin layer of foam. Try a flavoring suggested above. A Mocha Latte is made by substituting steamed chocolate milk for regular milk. Café Bailey's adds desired amounts of Irish Cream, crème de cacao and Frangelico.

The Flavor of Coffee

The source of the bean determines the quality of the coffee. Some of the better coffees are grown in Columbia, Costa Rica, El Salvador, Ethiopia, Guatemala, Hawaii, Sumatra, Kenya, Malawi, Panama and Papua New Guinea. These areas produce some of the world's best *arabica* beans, the preferred coffee bean.

The degree to which the coffee bean is roasted is decided by the roaster. The style of roast should bring out the most desirable qualities of a particular bean, and plays heavily in the flavor of coffee. There are four roasting styles, generally sold under a few names:

Light Roasts: Cinnamon and Half City
Medium Roasts: Full City, American, Regular and Breakfast
Dark Roasts: Contintal, New Orleans and Vienna
Darkest Roasts: French, Italian and Espresso

When selecting the bean, appreciate its scent and imagine what it will taste like when brewed. Characteristics of brewed coffee are:

Acidity: The acid content, a pleasant sharpness but not sour taste.
Aftertaste: The sensation that remains after swallowing.
Aroma: The scent of fruit, spice, nuts, wine, grassiness or burn.
Body: The richness or characteristics of the coffee on your palate.
Flavoring: The aromatics added after the final stage of roasting.
Mustiness: A lack of proper storage, may be present in aged beans.
Thin or Watery: Underbrewed coffee lacking acidity or coffee oils.

Mocha Coffee Cake

SERVES 8

2 egg whites
2 tablespoons canola oil
¾ cup sugar
1 teaspoon cinnamon
3 tablespoons coffee
1 teaspoon vanilla extract
8 oz. low-fat vanilla
    yogurt
1½ cups all-purpose flour
2 teaspoons baking
    powder
½ teaspoon baking soda
3 tablespoons sweetened
    cocoa powder

Crumb Topping:
3 tablespoons flour
3 tablespoons sugar
2 tablespoons finely
    chopped walnuts
1 teaspoon cinnamon
1 tablespoon butter,
    softened
2 teaspoons coffee

Position a rack in middle of oven and preheat to 350°. Spray a 9"x 9" cake pan with non-stick oil.

In a large bowl, beat egg whites, oil, sugar, cinnamon, coffee, vanilla and yogurt. Rest a strainer over the bowl. Sift and stir in flour, baking powder and baking soda. Pour one-third of the batter into prepared pan, sprinkle with 1½ tablespoons cocoa. Pour in half of the remaining batter, and sprinkle with remaining cocoa. Cover with remaining batter. Use a butter knife to make a few swirls in batter.

Combine dry topping ingredients. Use a fork to distribute butter and coffee, forming small crumbs. Sprinkle over batter. Bake 35 minutes. Cool 5 minutes in pan, then cut into squares.

The Coffee Bean

The coffee tree is actually a shrub which grows up to 10 meters (30 feet) tall. There are two commercial species - coffee *arabica* and *canephora* or *Robusta*. *Arabica* is the source of all fine coffees, and *robusta* an inexpensive blender, and the source of instant coffees. The plant is native to Ethiopia where it was discovered in the 15th century.

Coffee grows in a narrow band within 25° of the equator, at altitudes of 5,000 - 8,000 feet and temperatures of 50° - 70°. The fruit, called a cherry, ripens to a glossy red on the tree. After picking, the seed is removed from the fruit and dried in the sun. The outer covering of the seed is then removed, exposing the beans. The beans are graded, and can be stored for years on the plantation before being shipped to the roaster.

Roasting is the most important step in the production of coffee. Roasting breaks down the cell walls of the bean, allowing the aromatic oils and flavors to escape. By heating the beans to over 400°, roasting occurs in three phases; first the beans crack, then the starches are converted to sugar and carmelized to create the dark brown color, and finally the aromatic oils are forced to the surface of the bean. There are distinct roasting styles: light is most commonly used commercially, medium, dark and darkest. All are used with different kinds of beans to optimize their flavors and taste.

The Decaffeinated Experience

The obvious evening choice for those effected by the wakeful state of caffeine, and a growing choice of many concerned with the implications of high caffeine consumption, is decaffeinated coffee. Its growing popularity has encouraged coffee roasters to seek out better tasting and purer methods of decaffeination.

Decaffeination of the green coffee beans removes 96 to 98 percent of the caffeine, and is accomplished by one of two basic procedures. The first is to rinse the beans in a solvent which attaches itself to the caffeine, dry the beans, then remove the solvent. The second basic method is to continuously rinse the beans in water, flushing away the water soluble caffeine.

The direct method of decaffeination with a solvent generally employs methylene chloride which adheres to and dissolves the caffeine. Although the use of methylene chloride removes only the caffeine and none of the coffees' other properties, there are some growing environmental concerns about the use of this solvent. Variations on this method involve the use of other solvents and the use of water mixed with methylene chloride to rinse the beans.

The Swiss Water process uses "flavor-charged" water to rinse the beans and replace some of the coffee flavors flushed away. Another alternative is the natural process which uses a solvent that occurs in nature, other than water, to rinse away caffeine but not the flavor.

Irish Coffee

Per Cup:
1 teaspoon sugar
2 tablespoons Irish
    whiskey
¾ cup fresh brewed coffee
¼ cup low-fat whipped
    cream

In a large cup or glass, combine the sugar and whiskey. Stir in coffee. Top with whipped cream.

Café Marnier

SERVES 2

1 cup hot cocoa, made
    with skim milk
2 teaspoons sugar
1 cinnamon stick
4-inch strip orange peel
1½ cups fresh hot coffee
2 tablespoons Grand
    Marnier, Cointreau
    or Triplesec
4 tablespoons low-fat
    whipped cream

Make or heat hot cocoa in a medium saucepan. Add sugar and cinnamon stick, heat together for 5 minutes.

Remove from heat, stir in hot coffee and liqueur. Pour into tall glasses, topping each with 2 tablespoons whipped cream.

Apricot Scones

3 cups all-purpose flour,
plus flour for
kneading and rolling
1 tablespoon baking
powder
1 teaspoon baking soda
1 teaspoon cinnamon
¼ cup sugar
2 tablespoons butter,
softened
2 tablespoons safflower oil
1 cup finely chopped
dried apricots
1¼ cups low-fat
buttermilk
1 egg, beaten

MAKES 12

Preheat oven to 400°. In a large mixing bowl, combine flour, baking powder, baking soda, cinnamon and sugar. Using a fork or pastry cutter, cut in butter and oil until evenly distributed. Stir in dried apricots.

Briefly mix in buttermilk, just until moistened. Turn out onto floured board and lightly knead until dough becomes dry. Cut in half, pat each piece into a disk shape, and lightly roll into 7-inch circles.

Place circles on uncoated baking sheet, brush with beaten egg, and score each into 6 wedges. Bake 20 minutes, or until tops are golden. Serve warm or at room temperature.

Tea Time

While the Chinese are the true connoisseurs of tea, it is the English who made tea famous in Europe and the New World.

According to legend, the use of tea was discovered by the Chinese Emperor Shen Nong in 2737 B.C. Not until 1610 A.D. did the Dutch traders first bring tea to Europe. Tea leaves were so important that when the British imposed a tax on tea in 1767, it caused the American colonists to protest in the Boston Tea Party.

The English raised the tea experience to a social high. Afternoon tea, or tea time, developed in the early days of importing tea. Because tea was so expensive, only the elite could afford it so they created a social ceremony around the event. Gradually scones, cakes and sandwiches were added to complete the present day experience of tea time.

There is only one tea plant, but three basic types of tea - Black, green, and Oolong. The types are achieved by variations in the fermentation and drying process. Finer differentiations occur due to soil, locality, age of the plant, grading and blending. Tea is a major agricultural product of India, China, Japan, Pakistan and Sri Lanka. The plant matures in three to five years, as it produces new shoots containing a few leaves and a bud. Harvesters, called "plukers," select the tea shoots by hand.

English Tea

Directions for Making Tea: Empty the kettle, fill with fresh cold water, and put on to boil. Select a china or clay teapot and just before the water boils, pour a cup into the teapot, swirl to warm, then empty. Return kettle to heat.

English Tea requires the use of loose tea leaves, never tea bags. Place one heaping teaspoon of tea leaves per person into the pot, plus an extra teaspoon. If the leaves are a large variety and light for their volume, add one or two extra teaspoons. As soon as the water reaches a rolling boil, pour over the leaves, 1 cup per person. The tea will be brewed in three to six minutes, so check it frequently for darkness and strength. Just before serving, give the teapot one good stir. Pour tea through a strainer to catch the leaves. If you prefer tea with milk, add milk to cup before pouring tea. Sugar is not suggested, as it masks the full flavor of the tea.

Afternoon tea in London and the south of England is an elegant affair. A highlight of British society, afternoon tea is served in polished silver and fine china, accompanied by petits fours, finger sandwiches, scones, cakes, tea breads and spreads.

High tea is honored in the rural north of England and outlying areas of Scotland. Served around six o'clock in the evening with a pot of strong tea, it is a more robust affair with a hearty selection of meats, fish, country pies, eggs and filling pastries. High tea fills a country appetite after a long day.

Mint Tea with Crystallized Ginger

Per Cup:
1 tablespoon fresh leaves
   or 1 heaping teaspoon
   dried mint leaves
1 cup freshly boiled water
2 small pieces crystallized
   ginger

There are over a hundred varieties of mint. The most common brewing types are **peppermint, spearmint, apple mint, orange mint** and **Corsican mint.**

Place mint leaves in warmed teapot, and pour in water which has just begun to boil. Cover tea pot and steep 8-10 minutes.

Place crystallized ginger in tea cup. Strain leaves from tea while pouring into cup. The ginger will add a warming flavor and sweeten the tea.

This tea is both calming and rejuvinating. It will soothe a sore throat, upset stomach, headache and daily tensions. This is a lovely tea to prepare for a friend with a cold or allergies to help them breath easier.

Golden Raisin Tea Bread

½ cup almond slivers
¾ cup powdered sugar
¼ cup brown sugar
½ cup cake flour
¾ cup golden raisins
6 egg whites
3 tablespoons butter,
    melted
¼ cup skim milk

MAKES 2 MINI-BREADS

Preheat oven to 350°. Generously spray 2 mini-bread breads with non-stick oil.

In a blender or food processor, process almonds until finely ground. Add sugars and flour and pulse until well blended. Transfer to mixing bowl.

Mix in raisins, egg whites, melted butter and milk. Ladle into prepared pans and bake 15 minutes. Turn off oven, and leaves tea breads 5 minutes more in hot oven. Cool pans on rack for 10 minutes, invert to remove. Cool completely before slicing.

Roses and Cloves Tea

Be sure to use unsprayed rose petals and rose hips!

Per Cup:
2 teaspoons fresh deep red rose petals, or
1 teaspoon dried deep red petals, or
1 teaspoon ground rose hips, processed in a coffee grinder
3 whole cloves
1 cup boiling water
honey to taste

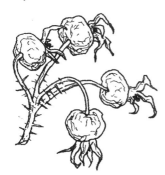

The petals from a deep red rose provide the best aroma and color, but other colors will also make excellent tea. If using a lighter colored rose, double the amount of petals.

Rose hips will give a fuller flavor if ground when dried, but can also be used fresh. They are very high in vitamin C, and have a refreshingly tart taste.

Place rose petals or ground hips in a warmed teapot with cloves. Just before water comes to a rolling boil, pour into teapot. (Using water just before it boils preserves vitamin C.) Cover pot and steep 8-10 minutes.

Strain off leaves while pouring into tea cups. Stir in honey to taste.

Burgundy Tea

3 cups water
4 black tea bags
1 cinnamon stick
3 whole cloves
rind of 1 orange
¼ cup sugar
1½ cups cranberry juice
1½ cups burgundy wine

SERVES 6

In a medium saucepan, boil water. Remove from heat and add tea bags, cinnamon stick, cloves and orange rind. Cover saucepan and let sit 5 minutes. Strain tea into another pot. Stir in sugar, cranberry juice and wine. Warm over medium heat.

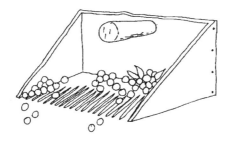

Orange Pekoe with a Twist

1 orange
3 loose tablespoons, or
    3 tea bags orange
    pekoe tea
4 cups boiling water
2 tablespoons Cointreau
    or Triplesec

milk, honey and/or sugar
    to taste

SERVES 4

Use a sharp knife to carefully peel long lengths of rind from orange. Cut into very thin strips of 3-4 inches in length. Take strips by the ends and twist to release oils.

Place orange twists with orange pekoe tea in a warmed tea pot or French press. Pour boiling water into tea pot or press. Cover and steep 5 minutes. Stir in Cointreau or Triplesec. Strain tea into cups with milk, honey or sugar as desired.

Selecting and Brewing Teas

Tea is sensitive to light, moisture, heat and time, so store it in air tight containers at room temperature. To brew, a few steps will ensure a delicious cup every time. Bring fresh cold water to a rolling boil. Pour over fresh tea leaves in a warmed teapot, cover and brew 3 - 5 minutes, stir once, then promptly strain the leaves.

Some teas have medicinal properties. Green teas are rich in fluoride and can reduce tooth decay, reduce bleeding and ease insect bites. Oolong tea keeps fats soluble in the body and reduces cholesterol. A compress made from Black tea will refresh tired eyes and ease sunburn.

Black teas include Darjeeling, Assam, Ceylon, Keemun and Lapsang Souchong. Oriental green teas are Gunpowder, Hyson, Gyokuro and Sencha. Popular blends available in most markets are English and Irish Breakfast, Russian, Earl Grey and Orchid.

Herbal teas can be made from Basil, Catnip, Chamomile, Chicory, Chrysanthemum, Ginger, Ginseng, Golden Seal, Hibiscus, Jasmine, Lavender, Lemon Verbena, Rose, Mint, Licorice, Lime, Peppermint, Parsley, Raspberry, Strawberry, Valerian, Yerba Mate, Angelica, Sage, Rosemary and Oregano.

Chamomile and Lemon Herb Tea

3 tablespoons fresh
   chamomile flowers, or
1 tablespoon dried
   chamomile

4 tablespoons fresh, or
1 tablespoon dried lemon
   balm

3 tablespoons fresh, or
1 tablespoon dried
   lemongrass

2 tablespoons finely
   chopped lemon rind
4½ cups boiling water
honey, preferably orange

SERVES 4

In a medium sized pot, combine herbs with lemon rind. Pour in water which has just begun to boil. Cover pot, set on low burner and steep 25 minutes. Strain off herbs while ladling into cups. Serve with honey.

Crumpets

1 pkg. dry yeast
2 teaspoons sugar
⅓ cup warm water
1¾ cups skim milk
2¼ cups all-purpose flour
½ teaspoon baking soda

1 tablespoons butter

To shape crumpets requires several 3-inch round cookie cutter rings. (Crumpets are similar to English muffins.)

MAKES 16

In a warmed mixing bowl, sprinkle yeast and sugar over warm water. Let rest 5 minutes. Stir in remaining ingredients, then cover with plastic wrap and let sit for 30 minutes.

Warm griddle over medium-high heat. Spray griddle with non-stick oil, then melt 1 teaspoon of butter on griddle. Spray cookie cutter rings with non-stick oil and place on hot griddle. Spoon about 3 tablespoons batter into each ring. Reduce heat to medium and cook until tops are full of holes. Remove the rings and, if desired, briefly brown on the other side.

Serve warm or toasted with jam or spread. Crumpets go well with a pot of hot tea.

Raspberry Tea Syrup & Herbal Tea Honey

RASPBERRY SYRUP:

2 cups water
¼ cup ginger root, thinly
    sliced
½ cup fresh chopped
    raspberry leaves or
    2 tablespoons raspberry
    tea leaves
1 tablespoon fresh grated
    lemon zest
1 cup sugar

This lovely syrup and honey will easily mix into hot or cold tea, adding interesting aromatic flavors and sweetness.

Raspberry Syrup: In a covered saucepan simmer ginger root, raspberry leaves and lemon zest for 15 minutes. Strain, then return to heat. Mix in sugar and simmer 20 minutes. Chill.

HERBAL HONEY:

8 oz. jar of honey
1 tablespoon dried mint
1 tablespoon dried
    lavender flowers
1 tablespoon ground rose
    hips or crushed hops

Herbal Honey: Combine all ingredients in a saucepan and warm 15 minutes over medium heat. Pour back into jar, seal and let set 1-2 weeks at room temperature. Place jar in hot bowl of water until honey has thinned, then pour through strainer to remove herbs.

Hazelnut Hot Cocoa

4 cups skim milk
4-6 tablespoons
    unsweetened Dutch
    process cocoa powder
4 tablespoons sugar
4 drops vanilla extract
½ teaspoon hazelnut
    extract, or
2 tablespoons Frangelico

low-fat whipped cream

SERVES 4

In a medium pot, stir cocoa powder and sugar into cold milk. Heat over medium-low heat until liquid is steaming. Remove from heat, stir in vanilla, and hazelnut extract or Frangelico. Serve hot in mugs topped with whipped cream.

Almond Biscotti

2 cups sifted all-purpose
    flour
½ teaspoon baking soda
¼ teaspoon salt
2 eggs
⅜ cup sugar
⅜ cup packed light brown
    sugar
½ teaspoon vanilla extract
½ teaspoon almond
    extract
½ cup chopped almond
    slivers

MAKES 4-5 DOZEN COOKIES

Preheat the oven to 300°F. Line baking sheet with parchment paper.

Whisk flour, baking soda and salt in a small bowl. In a medium bowl, beat eggs with sugars, vanilla and almond extract. Briefly beat in flour mixture, then stir in nuts.

Use a large spoon to scoop batter onto baking sheet, dividing it into three long, skinny 12-inch ropes, 2½-inches apart. Neaten the edges. Bake for 35 minutes. Cool 10 minutes on pan, then peel from paper and place on cutting board. Slice into ½-inch thick pieces and place on two cookie sheets, leaving space between cookies. Bake 10 minutes, turn biscotti and bake 10 minutes more. Cool before storing in airtight container.

Mulled Apple Cider

1 quart apple cider
8 cloves and/or cardamon
    seeds
5-inch cinnamon stick

MAKES 1 QUART

Heat all ingredients well, at least 30 minutes, but do not boil. Strain off spices when serving. Store unused portion in refrigerator. Mulled cider can be reheated, or served cold.

Note: The longer spices are in the cider the stronger the flavor will be.

Chai

3 cups water
3 tea bags black or
    Darjeeling tea
2 cinnamon sticks
8 cardamon seeds
4 whole cloves
3 tablespoons sugar
2 cups skim milk
1 cup non-fat powdered
    milk

SERVES 4

Boil water in a kettle. Place tea bags, cinnamon sticks, cardamon seeds and cloves in a pot, and pour in boiling water. Cover pot, simmer on medium-low heat for 5 minutes. Uncover pot, reduce heat to low and leave untouched for 15 minutes.

Strain to remove tea bags, cinnamon sticks and cardamon seeds. Return tea to pot and stir in sugar, skim milk and non-fat powdered milk. To serve, heat thoroughly, without boiling.